DISCARD

Dedicated to Summer. When you were a little girl,
I loved reading you picture books. Writing one together
is a dream come true. Reading or writing, I love you.

—MB

Dedicated to my little cousins. May you take hold
of the things that inspire you and find God
speaking through them.

—SBD

God
Speaks
in
Whispers

MARK BATTERSON *and*
SUMMER BATTERSON DAILEY

illustrated by **Benedetta Capriotti**

Big sound,
little sound,
where in the world
is God's voice found?

Can you hear God crashing in the *waves?*

Can you hear Him **e c h o** in the caves?

Do you hear Him when a bird chirps?

Or when your sister slurps?

Can you hear Him on **TOP** of a mountain?
Or even at the drinking fountain?

Do you hear God's voice

when you're feeling sad?

Or perhaps when you're
a little **_mad_**?

God speaks through stars
that shoot through the sky.

God speaks in whispers as *soft* as a sigh.

Why is God whispering
so you barely hear?
It's really quite simple:
you have to get near!

Sort of like Grandma,
who gives you a hug
or tucks you in bed,
all nice and snug.

God whispers down deep to the depths of your **heart,**
"I've been with you from the very start."

God speaks through His Word,
so you know what is right.

God speaks in dreams, by day and by night.

God speaks through nature,

like a big blue glacier.

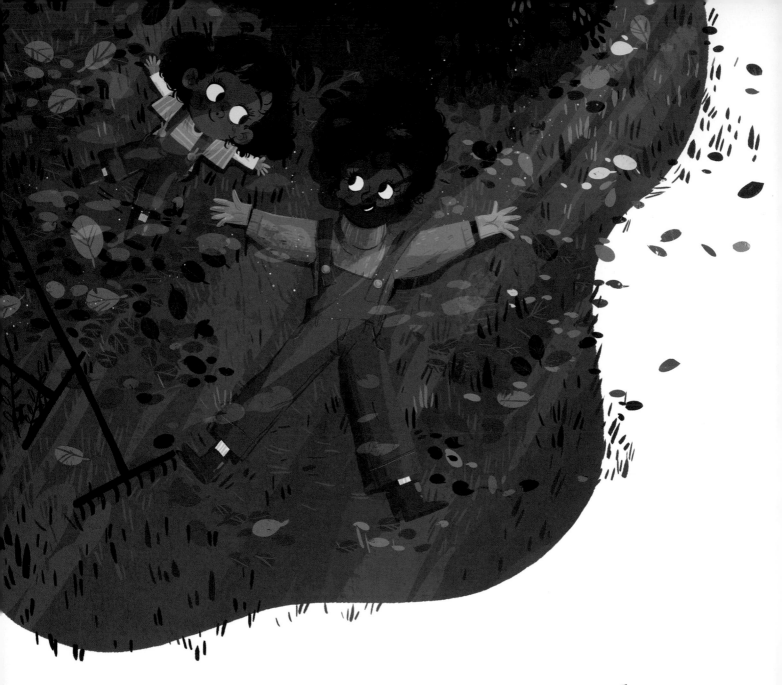

God speaks through family and friends, and so much more, sometimes right in the middle of a chore!

Just like waves that speak for the ocean
or friends who make quite the **commotion.**

God points the way for you to go.
God whispers things you need to know.

He says what is true,
that you can be you,
even in all of
your hullabaloo.

Late at night, after you close your eyes
and long before it's time to rise,

God is present, God is waiting,
God is even re-creating.

So when you wake up to a world that's spinning,
jump out of bed, get dressed, start grinning!

For God's whisper is in your smile,
a smile even **bigger** than a **crocodile**!

Some days are filled with lots of fun, like running and jumping and playing in the sun.

Mom tickles your tummy
and makes you wiggle,
until you let out a **great big** *giggle!*

But even on days
that aren't so good,
days when you don't feel
heard or understood,

your feelings, they matter,
even if they're all mixed up like
pancake batter.

God is speaking, **rain** or **shine**.
God is loving all the time.

Remember that God is still right here,
listening to every single prayer!

Above all else,

know this is true,

that God is singing
all around you.

And what is He saying in that voice, still and small?

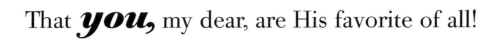

That **you,** my dear, are His favorite of all!

GOD SPEAKS IN WHISPERS

Hardcover ISBN 978-0-525-65385-1
eBook ISBN 978-0-525-65386-8

Text copyright © 2020 by Mark Batterson and Summer Batterson
Illustrations copyright © 2020 by Benedetta Capriotti

Cover design by Patrice Sheridan; cover illustration by Benedetta Capriotti

Published in the United States by Multnomah, an imprint of Random House, a division of Penguin Random House LLC.

MULTNOMAH® and its mountain colophon are registered trademarks of Penguin Random House LLC.

Library of Congress Cataloging-in-Publication Data
Names: Batterson, Mark, author. | Batterson, Summer, author.
Title: God speaks in whispers / Mark Batterson and Summer Batterson.
Description: Colorado Springs, Colorado : Multnomah, 2020.
Identifiers: LCCN 2019047665 | ISBN 9780525653851 (hardcover) | ISBN 9780525653868 (ebook)
Subjects: LCSH: God (Christianity)—Juvenile literature.
Classification: LCC BT107 .B38 2020 | DDC 231.7—dc23
LC record available at https://lccn.loc.gov/2019047665

Printed in China

2020—First Edition

10 9 8 7 6 5 4 3 2 1

SPECIAL SALES
Most Multnomah books are available at special quantity discounts when purchased in bulk by corporations, organizations, and special-interest groups. Custom imprinting or excerpting can also be done to fit special needs. For information, please email specialmarketscms@penguinrandomhouse.com.